HEAT

T0362593

Series 3 Number 5

Jacqueline Rose
Vertical Thoughts 2017
ink and collage on paper

Jacqueline Rose is exhibiting at
Woollahra Gallery at Redleaf in
Sydney from 30 November 2022 to
8 January 2023.

JENNY ERPENBECK
THINGS THAT DISAPPEAR

Translated by Kurt Beals

Jenny Erpenbeck, born in East Berlin in 1967, is the author of several works of fiction including *The Book of Words*; *The Old Child*; *Visitation*; *The End of Days*; *Go, Went, Gone*; and *Kairos*, recently published in German and forthcoming in English in 2023. These works of fiction, along with her collection of essays, *Not a Novel*, have been published in the United States by New Directions and in the United Kingdom by Granta. For her works, translated into thirty languages, she has won prizes including the Thomas Mann Prize (Germany), the Premio Strega (Italy) and the Lee Hochul Prize (South Korea). She lives with her family in Berlin.

Kurt Beals is Associate Professor of German and Comparative Literature at Washington University in St. Louis. Beals has translated a wide range of works from German into English, most recently *Franz Kafka: The Drawings* by Andreas Kilcher and Pavel Schmidt. His translation of Jenny Erpenbeck's speech and essay collection *Not a Novel* was included in *World Literature Today*'s '75 Notable Translations of 2020'.

Memories

The farewells are what I remember. How thin and white R. looked beneath his shock of hair when I said goodbye to him for the last time and he nodded to me without lifting his head from the pillow, just briefly closing his eyes. How I didn't go back to his bed, but simply closed the door behind me. The next day I had to pick up his things from the hospital, including the razor I'd charged for him the day before. The razor was charged, but R. was dead.

When I left my grandmother's house, she was standing at the window of a dark room, waving as I walked away, her silhouette illuminated only by the light that burned behind her in the hallway where we had just said our goodbyes. Two days later she fell, and when I saw her again, her face motionless and her eyes closed, she was lying in a coma in the hospital, where some time later she died.

I remember how R. would nod after he had examined something – a car, a new apartment – I remember how he would hum along under his breath when there was gypsy music playing in a Hungarian restaurant, I remember how he would hunch his shoulders when he was carrying a tray back to the kitchen. I still recall how my grandmother used to say 'Oh dear, oh dear' when she was in a hurry and didn't know what to do first, I remember her hands with their gnarled fingernails and her laughter. I already find it hard to recall whether her mouth was open or closed when she laughed, but at least I know how it sounded, and how her laughter gradually faded into laughter at herself.

There's very little that I can touch, see and hear with my memory anymore. The thoughts of someone who no longer exists can be translated into my thoughts, and the actions of that person into my actions, but the tangible part of those memories will probably fall to pieces sooner or later. When reality no longer grows back, it will become a skeleton, individual bones with a great deal of soil in between. Recently, it's often happened that I find myself sitting across from someone who's still perfectly alive, yet looking at him as if he had already disappeared. At those moments, half hopeful, half ashamed, I pick out single frames of the film while it's still running, as if I could select my memories in advance and learn them by heart, so that I could be sure to recall them later. As for myself, I've already considered whether anyone will remember the way I blow my nose, or the way I watch a boxing match on TV, or my knees.

Miezel

On the way to see Maria, known as Miezel, I have to drive through the valley, first down to the lowest and coldest point along the route – the road makes a sharp curve there, so it's easy to skid in the winter – then back up at the other end of the valley, then a right at the Kreuzwirt tavern, past the forest that Miezel helped plant thirty years ago – at night you can often see deer in the meadow that borders the forest, standing there as if petrified, blinded by the headlights. Today, in the sunlight, I see two figures coming toward me there: an overweight mother with her equally overweight, grown-up daughter, holding each other's hands.

The journey to see Miezel has become a very long one since I moved back to Berlin. Hunched over like a crescent moon, her silhouette approaches the frosted glass panes of the door. Then Maria, known as Miezel, opens the door to me. In the time I've known her, she's grown ever thinner and more frail. Still, her hair is only grey in a few places. She wears an apron over her skirt,

10

and slippers on her feet because of the corns. 'Pain,' she says, and smiles, 'constant pain!' – she smiles and shakes her head as if in amazement, her feet are bony like the rest of her body, and whenever she bumps into anything her skin immediately turns blue in that spot, since the veins are just beneath the surface.

Miezel lives in the castle where she served as a maid all her life, on the ground floor, right next to the entrance. Until just a few years ago, she was still carrying suitcases up to the third floor. She cooked, cleaned and tended the garden for the masters of the estate. She opens the door for guests, workmen, the chimney sweep and the postman. The bricklayer and the gardener take their lunch break in her kitchen. Miezel drinks raspberry syrup mixed with tap water, she cooks her food on an iron stove, and any leftover provisions that aren't suitable for the compost are thrown onto the fire. Miezel has never flown in an airplane. She always used to walk the three kilometres to the village on foot, back before she started to get dizzy so often. She never learned to ride a bicycle, and never used an escalator. When the masters aren't at home, she tends the castle, and her only companions are the dormouse, the Aesculapian snake and the red salamander. The house where she was born is at the foot of the hill where the castle stands. Miezel can see it from her window.

One of the two rooms she's lived in for thirty years is the front parlour. She keeps fruit and cake there in a cool and shady place, baskets and trays are laid out on a huge black table with lathe-turned legs that once belonged to someone or other who lived in these rooms before. The other room is the one where Miezel sleeps, her dresses and aprons are hung there in a shallow closet, and there's a TV, too, and an armchair, its upholstery already worn rather bare in the spots where Miezel places her hands on the armrests. She brings in the coffee pot, and I can see that a coffee pot like that holds weight.

Back when I was her neighbour, she would always carry something in her hands when she came to visit me – a head of lettuce, or two or three apples, or some mushrooms, or a plate of cakes. 'A few Buchteln,' she'd say, Austrian sweet rolls. The things she brought were things she'd planted, cooked, baked or found in the woods herself. Later, when she couldn't go into the woods or work in the garden anymore, or even cook or bake, she made me open-faced sandwiches. White bread with cheese or salami, with slices of egg or halved sour pickles on top. She arranged the slices of egg on the bread with her bony hands, and if I didn't manage to eat it all, I had to take the rest home with me wrapped in aluminum foil – for this evening, for tomorrow – along with a package of cookies for my child.

When I ring her doorbell today, it's a long time before the door is opened. Her caretaker must not be very familiar with the keys yet. High up in the sky, far above the big cherry tree, a hawk is circling. Inside, in her dimly lit kitchen, Miezel is seated at the table; her caretaker has set her there and pushed the chair close to the table so that she can hold herself upright. Miezel sits there, but she's so weak that she can't even manage to open her eyes. I look out her window. Through the bare trees, I can see as far as the house where her mother was a maid and her father was a servant. Miezel sits there motionless. That means that when I leave, I can only hug her from the side.

Cheese and Socks
The other day I bought some cheese, a particularly expensive piece of cheese, I cut myself a slice while I was standing in front of

the refrigerator, and it tasted very good. That same evening, the piece of cheese was nowhere to be found – not in the refrigerator, or in any of the cabinets, or on the table, or in the freezer, or even in the toolbox, in the washing machine, in the linen closet, or on the balcony. Not in the oven, either. In fact, it had really and truly disappeared, and it stayed that way, too, it had disappeared so thoroughly that it didn't even start to stink after a while from any corner that I might have forgotten about while searching for my piece of cheese. I ask my mother, who knows her way around my house: Have you by any chance seen the cheese? She says no. I say: Did you by any chance throw it away? My mother says no.

The same thing happened to my son with the little book that we kept in the bathroom to read aloud from during his longer visits: *How to Survive Situations You'll Probably Never Get Into.* It included instructions on how to fend off a crocodile, a shark, and a cougar, how to climb from a motorcycle into a car while driving, what to do if your parachute doesn't open, and so forth. We spent a lot of time studying that little book, so much time that I got quite tired of the page with the shark and preferred to roll down the windows while driving across a frozen lake to balance the water pressure in case of sinking – then it would be a piece of cake to get out of the car at the bottom of the lake. But suddenly that little book has disappeared. It isn't on the bookshelf, it isn't mixed in with the waste paper, it hasn't slipped behind the radiator or into the basket with the dirty laundry. I ask my mother: Have you by any chance seen our little yellow book? She says no.

Third, a single sock disappears, half of my favourite pair, but that's not at all unusual. I've heard that in probability theory there's a law concerning this very phenomenon (the Greek word for 'appearance'): the law of disappearing socks. And this brings me to my hope. My hope that the disappearance of things in one place necessarily results in their appearance in another place, that there may be a world in which my sock, filled with that expensive piece of cheese, plunges from a very high bridge and survives the fall.

Friend

Now I'm going to make you disappear in this column. It's as simple as that. In you go. But why, my friend asks. That's what I'm asking you, I say. What's this all about, she says. Yes, I say, that's what I'd like to know, too. In you go, I say, then shut the lid, then everything is calm and quiet. Calm and quiet sometimes occur in friendships, and there are different kinds: the calm after the storm, the calm before the storm, or simply calm. This last sort of calm has something to do with the disappearance of the friendship, that much is certain; perhaps this calm is not calm at all, but silence, and perhaps this silence itself is the cause of the silence, in which case the disappearance would be something circular.

When I'm riding my bike, little insects sometimes fly into my mouth or up my nose. And before I know it, they're in my throat, and my throat gulps them down, and there's nothing I can do but try after the fact to think of the insects as food, so that it doesn't bother me that they've ended up inside me. In the case of one of those little flies or mosquitoes, you could certainly say that it disappeared into my mouth or nose, but really it's still there, just out of sight. Whenever a little mosquito or fly disappears into my mouth and my throat gulps it down against my will, I ask myself whether just slipping out of sight is enough in itself to count as disappearance, or whether a more thorough dissolution is required.

The other question that inevitably occurs to me each time something disappears is whether anything was there to begin with – and if so, what. In the case of a friendship, for example, which is invisible from the start, it may be that the bond whose disappearance I mourn was only an appearance anyway, that in essence there were just two lonely quantities of the most eclectic odds and ends that overlapped for a while and are now drifting apart again.

The most encouraging reading would be that the more thoroughly a friendship disappears, the more securely it is preserved. That silence takes up just as much space and connects us just as firmly to one another as all the walks, conversations, shopping trips, afternoons spent at playgrounds, glasses of wine and cups of coffee put together. That the answers that were not given remain faithful to me, through their absence, for all eternity. That although the disappearance has entered my body against my will, in retrospect it can be seen as nourishment, at least until I have had my fill.

Men

For a few weeks there was a strong smell of cats emanating from the middle apartment on the third floor, then it grew into a stench, the windows in the hallway were left wide open during the day and even at night, and finally the animal welfare agency, acting on a tip from some neighbours, broke down the door and freed three cats that had gone mad – two more already had their insanity behind them, they were dead. On occasions like that, the animal welfare men wear helmets made of metal mesh, as if they were dressed for fencing, because the abandoned animals in their rage make no distinction between one person and another. The cats' owner, it was said, had probably simply forgotten about his animals.

In Wagner's Ring cycle, the forgetful hero Siegfried, wrapped in his airy invisibility cloak, travels swiftly from marriage to marriage; today he would probably be called a marriage swindler. The man is already thundering down the stairs, fleeing across the courtyard, when the woman shouts after him: 'Get out!' – as if these words, of all things, could persuade her beloved to stay. The fact that disappearing from one place means appearing in another can hardly be shown more beautifully than in the film *The Man Who Walked Through the Wall*, in which the tax official Buchsbaum (Heinz Rühmann) discovers one day that he is able to pass in and out of closed rooms, to move through walls as if through water. In essence, he disappears from his life as a third-tier tax official and reappears as a supernatural being. Rarely has the change of circumstances, or the change of state that necessarily accompanies the disappearance and reappearance of both people and things, gone more smoothly.

An acquaintance of mine had a child who was only three months old when her husband told her he was leaving. Then he left. Thirteen years later, he came back and befriended his daughter. Another friend had phases like that in her life, too, sometimes the moon was in its first quarter, sometimes it was full, sometimes it wasn't visible at all. The father of her child had actually acknowledged his son in advance, but he never made an appearance after the birth. When the child was one and a half, the father unexpectedly showed up at the door. For a few months he played with his son, went on outings, and even bought a Christmas tree. Then he disappeared as suddenly as he had come, and he has not been seen again; the child is seven now. In any case, disappearance is surely no less powerful than love, but it remains astonishing that thin air can sometimes have just as much weight as something that is really there.

Disassembly

We are only guests on earth, we've known that for a long time, but even before we vacate the premises altogether, we are guests time and again, as if for a trial run: in other people's apartments, summer houses, hotels. Before we vacate the premises altogether and all our baggage inevitably falls away, we have the opportunity to transport our earthly belongings to this place or that, as we please. At some point, when the time is up, a woman may come, or a man, or an owner, or a landlord, and tell us to disappear. It's also possible for us to disappear before we're asked to. Or to disappear reluctantly, and belatedly. Finally, it's possible for us to be gone before anyone has even noticed that we were there to begin with, so that our disappearance goes entirely unnoticed. But wherever we stay, for however short or long a time, we always, at a minimum, open a door, go inside, breathe, perhaps sit on a chair, eat from plates, drink from glasses, sleep in beds, we may stock up on essentials, play games, browse through books, move the rug a bit when we go out, turn the key only once when we lock up, instead of twice as the owner of the house usually does. We bring some things with us, we handle others, move them just a bit, or our smell clings to them, but in any case, when we disappear, our things are supposed to disappear as well, the mark we've made is supposed to be taken back and disappear along with us, then we have to drag all our belongings from the apartments, the houses, the rooms that we leave, the way an octopus drags its tentacles from an undersea cave.

And that's why this weekend I'm standing on a teetering platform in the branches of an oak tree, pounding on the boards of a tree house with a hammer to pry them loose, that's why I'm using a pipe wrench to unscrew the hammock hooks from tree trunks full of resin, the pipe wrench breaks and it all blows up in my face, that's why I'm deflating balls, folding chairs and tables, wrapping plates and glasses in newspaper, that's why I'm stuffing jackets and sweaters into suitcases, rubber boots and ice skates into a big bag, that's why I'm even digging up my peony at the very last minute. When you leave a hotel, you often see the doors of the rooms that have already been vacated standing open, revealing rumpled sheets, empty bottles, crumpled paper, cigarette butts and ashes. Now the rented place where we spent four summers doesn't look much different than those abandoned hotel rooms. As I'm driving away, I can barely fit into the car because so many things have become attached to me and have to disappear with me when I leave.

OLIVER DRISCOLL
TWO SIMPLE STORIES
ABOUT FRIENDSHIP

Oliver Driscoll is the author of the poetry collection *I Don't Know How That Happened* (2020), and *White Clouds Blue Rain* (2021), which is made up of a series of triptychs, each with a work a poetry, a piece of essayistic prose, and a photographic image. He won the 2015 Lord Mayor's Award for Narrative Nonfiction and was shortlisted for the 2019 Dorothy Hewett Award for an Unpublished Manuscript. Oliver lives in Melbourne where he co-runs the *Slow Canoe* live journal and chapbook press.

The Famous Friendship

Lily and Tom met at university. Quickly they became friends but never anything more. They had gone to the same high school but were so different then that they'd hardly had anything to do with each other. A few weeks after he turned forty, a time when they were both single and feeling a little bit alone, Tom said, why don't we just give it a go and move in together. Lily blushed and squeezed his hand. After several weeks had passed and he was yet to hear a word from Lily, Tom was surprised and relieved to find that he still didn't feel overly compelled to call or message her.

Both Lily and Tom were taking a double History–English major but after three years, in a panic, Lily switched over to graphic design, something Tom hadn't realised she was interested in. Through his final year, he felt her absence acutely. It seemed to Tom that Lily was at university forever, and so long as she was, he felt as though he could live as though he was still there himself, but even before she graduated she was offered a job at a design firm. When she completed her final semester and started working full-time at the firm, she suddenly had substantially more money than either of them had ever had before. She seemed to enjoy being able to come over to Tom's apartment with takeaway and wine and say, it's fine, don't worry about it, I waive the debt. But just when this seemed as though it would become a permanent state, one they were both comfortable with, Lily realised how little she liked her job. She'd genuinely cared about history, that sense of living amongst greater units of time and the odd feeling of newly discovering that which was anything but new. She should never have given it up so easily.

She started to look into other options, like the conservation of artworks and artefacts. She could do a master's. Tom said he'd never understood why she'd changed courses. She said, you didn't say anything at the time. You wouldn't have listened, he said, and besides, you never brought it up, you just went and changed courses, you didn't want me to say anything. Lily was playfully forlorn. You can be sad in your little raincoat, he said, in reference to a scene from a film they'd watched together some years earlier. You can be sad in your little raincoat, Lily repeated softly, as it was one of the things that was always repeated. In the film, two hard-faced Russian children, a boy and a girl, had stood by a roadside in the sleet wearing matching green plastic raincoats bawling uncontrollably.

A year or so after Tom had graduated, when Gemma first stayed over his place, he told Lily about it, going into somewhat more detail here and there than he ever thought he would have. He immediately felt guilty towards both Gemma and Lily for having spoken so openly, and right then and there he apologised to Lily. Lily said there was nothing for him to apologise for, they were friends, she hoped they could talk about anything, particularly relationships. When Lily started dating Marcin, however, Tom didn't know Marcin even existed for weeks. Suddenly Lily and Marcin were there being very familiar with each other like an established couple.

There were times when Tom thought that friendship was the greater test, but most of the time, he thought you never knew if you could really put up with a person until you lived together, shared a bed, and saw each other more or less every day. One thing that Lily said to him early on, during that fabulous but confusing first year when there was so much that passed between them, was that while people talk about being able to get away with lying, it's much harder to be able to get away with being honest. I want to know how to be honest, she said, when it's the right time to be, and to not feel the need to be when it doesn't matter so much, to know how to hold myself back. Over time, Tom came to suspect that when she couldn't be straight with him, she just wouldn't say anything at all, even if this meant not seeing him for a while. He was deeply frustrated by this but he greatly admired her resolve. He wished he didn't have to take her judgement so seriously. Throughout much of the year he'd seen Gemma, Lily had been impossible to see.

With James, Lily had become enthusiastic about outdoor rock climbing and trail running. She'd never been particularly active before, though she'd always jogged and swam a little, but now she was wearing colourful trail shoes and hooded stretchy tops. She hadn't seemed to Tom like someone who would follow a partner in this way but he enjoyed seeing it unfold. You should come climbing with us, she said, you have the perfect body type, slim and strong. She described a wall of granite that she, James and some friends of theirs had recently climbed. James was quiet and well-mannered and easy to be around. It wasn't difficult to imagine him quietly gliding up a rock face but Tom never joined them and never saw them climb.

Lily was close to both of her parents but not particularly close to her siblings, a brother and a sister. For Tom it was the other way around. Tom only saw Lily's brother, who would come around on a bright green motorbike with 'Ninja' written in flashy purple and red writing on the side, when she was moving house and needed a hand.

When Lily invited Tom to her sister's wedding, he asked her if he was her plus-one or whether he should bring someone. She said, bring someone. But he'd only recently split up with Gemma, which had involved her moving out of the apartment they'd shared, that she'd just moved into a couple of months earlier, and he didn't feel like finding a date.

Occasionally, not often, Tom wished he could touch the bridge of Lily's nose, in much the same way he had liked to gently run the heel of his thumb across the closed eyes of his family's cats.

In order to have enough time to take on a master's, Lily moved to a smaller graphic design firm where she could work two or three days a week. Tom could see she was working much harder at her studies than she had during either of her undergraduate degrees. She became particularly interested in the preservation and restoration of paper. She said to him that you go into this course thinking you're going to be mostly interested in the history, but it's the chemistry that's really fascinating. Everything, oxygen, anything you might touch the artefact with, could be damaging or could leave a trace. She said she enjoyed having to fight against her nature in order to be as slow and meticulous as the work required. Well, she went on, hopefully being slow and meticulous truly is my nature.

Lily took time off work to go on a big camping trip with Tom. They hired a camper and drove up the coast. Tom enjoyed their rhythm. They would set up the van, cook on a gas stove, brush their teeth while passing a water bottle back and forth, and they would do long and sometimes quite difficult day walks.

Lily was still very fit and they pushed each other on the walks and were often ready to collapse by the time they returned to the van. Tom would be dripping with sweat. A few nights into the trip, they set up their camper not far from a group of men, by a big rocky creek. After Lily and Tom went to bed on the foam mattresses in the van, they could still hear the rowdy men laughing and jeering and even occasionally singing. Tom could feel that Lily was squirming around next to him. It was as though if he were to gently touch her arm she would collapse into him. Why then, he wondered, did he not want to touch her arm. Are you awake, she asked, and he said nothing.

Lily didn't enjoy her first conservation job, which was at a regional gallery that she had to drive to and from every day. She complained about a domineering older woman who was always making remarks about the quality of work of various employees behind their backs.

From Rhodes, Lily emailed Tom to say that she'd met a handsome British man, Paul, who was cycling around Europe. She was going to apply for a visa so she could go back to Brighton with him. But then a month later she was home. She said to Tom that she refused to get over this one. She could feel him in her veins and she wanted him there. A few weeks after this she told Tom that she and Paul were emailing and she was doing her best to convince him that he was wrong.

Lily's grandfather, who she wanted nothing to do with for reasons that were never clear to Tom, turned up a few times asking to see her at her second and much better conservation job at a major museum. The museum was right near the studio apartment her grandfather kept in the city. Being a new job it was uncomfortable having to explain to the person at the desk that she couldn't come out and see the man.

Each time, she was left flustered and unable to really concentrate for the rest of the day. Once, through a small window, she watched him confidently striding away from the counter, holding a baseball cap by the brim.

During a lunchbreak at the museum café, Lily said to Tom that she'd finally learned how to dress herself. It's about the balance between masculine and feminine, she said, but I've also come to accept that I look good in creams and pale blue. She said there was a swathe of time where she was apparently trying to dress like a five-year-old boy. I hope, she said, that in the future I'll look back at that time more fondly than I do now. Tom enjoyed these lunches at the museum café, particularly as he would wander around the museum store afterwards, looking at all the well-designed products on sale that he would never want nor need. But their time together was always too brief, and Lily always had a rushed air about her.

When time was up, Tom remained seated at the café table from where he watched Lily disappear further into the museum. There was the chatter, and the chiming of porcelain and metal of the café as well as the faint hollow echo of the museum atrium just beyond the next table, and there was the brighter lighting of the store that Tom would soon be walking through a little way away.

False Starts and New Beginnings

Mary worked for a chiropractor across the street from where Rebecca lived with her parents in a little three-bedroom cottage. The chiropractor, Sophie, lived down the back, away from the practice, but it was in her kitchen that Mary prepared lunch for herself every day. The kitchen was teal and soft grey, like the parts of the house given over to the practice, and the logo on Sophie's business card.

Mary saw Rebecca around the neighbourhood a number of times, particularly at the café on the corner with the blue steps, before they got to talking. Mary would have guessed she was nearer to her own age, twenty-five, not seventeen. Rebecca, it turned out, was still at high school, in her final year. Rebecca was very beautiful, Mary thought, and even more beautiful as you got to know her. Sophie once referred to Rebecca as Mary's South American friend, but that's not where Rebecca's family was from. Her mother was French and her father was from Granada, where he'd been some kind of roller disco champion. On her laptop, Rebecca showed Mary scans of photographs of him wearing bright yellow skates, and a matching headband holding his hair up.

Rebecca was planning to study fine art the following year and would stay up late, almost to sunrise, more or less every night drawing and painting. Mostly she would copy from a book of black-and-white photographs of women. Mary didn't think much of the finished products. The women's facial features were too heavily worked so they looked a little like masks, their fingers long and bony, and their breasts just a little bit too rounded. Rebecca never seemed to commit to blackening the images sufficiently to match the photographs. One afternoon, Mary commented that the way we see and represent is broadly influenced by the culture we happen to be a part of. She said, we're a little bit trapped, aren't we. No, Rebecca said, I'm not influenced by anyone. Mary could tell that she wouldn't be able to push the point any further without a fight. But all the same, she found herself frequently going over there after work. They'd make a simple dinner or walk down the road to get burgers or pizzas, and then return to Rebecca's room. Mary would lie on the bed, flicking through books and magazines while Rebecca painted and drew. Occasionally Mary would stay over and try to make herself look fresh in the same clothes at work the next morning. Rebecca said that her mum had sensed that Mary must be very good at building things with her hands. Mary had no idea if this were true, but she agreed all the same. On one evening, Rebecca took a photograph of the two of them sitting on the bed surrounded by pillows. When she plugged the camera cable into her laptop to see it, she said, severely, I once saw you before we met. It had been at a gallery opening and Mary had given her exactly the look she had in the photograph. Rebecca said she'd only ever seen men look at her like that. It took Mary over an hour to smooth things over.

Mary was never sure if she'd stick with the job. Sophie seemed to be watching her or to be somehow aware of her as she walked around the house and practice, and would eat her food from the fridge. If Mary were to ask Sophie about the missing food, she would say it must have been on the wrong shelf, that she would never touch anything that was Mary's. Rebecca had started selling things at the local market, mostly old op-shop purses she'd stick things to and bracelets she'd made out of old lace, pieces of fabric and buttons. The bracelets looked surprisingly good on her but when she gave one to Mary she was a little bit embarrassed by it. Mary tried to suppress the feeling and to keep wearing the bracelet but she simply couldn't.

The two of them started spending time with Mary's friend Jack. When they went to the beach Mary realised she'd only ever seen Rebecca dressed in clothes that covered her arms down to her wrists, and much of her legs. Now she was sitting in Jack's car wearing cut-off jeans and a singlet. Afterwards Jack dropped Mary off first. The following afternoon, Mary asked Rebecca about her clothing, and the long sleeves. Rebecca said that in the early part of high school, looking the way she did, she attracted a lot of attention and ended up in situations she hadn't later been happy about. Dressing the way she did was her response to all that, she said. You know, she said, I haven't even kissed a boy in years, even though you'd hardly believe the stuff that happened before then. Last night, she said, we went back to the beach and I so wanted to but was too frightened, and for once the guy, your friend Jack, had been too considerate to do anything himself. Mary felt her blood boil. She could just imagine the dark beach, the black and silvery water and the cool sand.

Rebecca didn't go off to university to study fine art the following year. She said she wanted to hang around awhile to get her bearings. She took a job at the café on the corner, where they were kind enough to make a little space where she could sell her pictures, bracelets and purses. Every so often something would sell, and Rebecca would be overjoyed. It's such a special feeling, she said to Mary. Mary was no longer upset about Jack and now enjoyed spending time with the two of them. Their age difference, she decided, wasn't really a big deal. For the time being, Jack painted houses. It was easy work but, he said, you got bored of it pretty quickly. If you didn't distract yourself with the radio, you just thought about how long until this wall was finished and then the next wall and then it was back to the first wall. Rebecca said he should be proud of the work he's doing. He's brightening up people's lives.

The three of them would go out drinking together. One evening, after a few drinks at a bar overlooking the beach, Rebecca took off through the unlit scrub of trees between the houses and the sand. Mary and Jack went after her but when they caught up to her she said, I don't need your protection. She took off again and again they caught up to her and asked her to come back to the bar with them. What's wrong, Mary asked. She said to them that nothing was wrong and that the two of them should just go back and have a drink. You get along so well together, she said. Besides, you're the same age, I'm just a kid. The three of them started walking back to the bar but then Rebecca slipped away again. Mary couldn't care less anymore and she could see that Jack couldn't either. The two of them walked silently back to their table at the bar and sat down. A couple of minutes later Rebecca reappeared through the darkness with a translucent snakeskin draped across her open palms. Look, she said. The next time Mary was over at Rebecca's house, she saw that Rebecca had painted a portrait of herself and had stuck the snakeskin across the hands of the image in just the way she'd been carrying it.

Jack, it turned out, had been sleeping with a friend of his, just casually, all along. A mutual friend of his and Mary's accidentally mentioned it to Mary and there it was. When

Rebecca confronted him, Jack denied it for a second and then he simply said, well, that's that then. For a few days Rebecca was a little irritable, but then while she and Mary were watching a movie together in her room on the laptop, she started sobbing and Mary held her. There wasn't anything to do or say. They let the movie run.

Rebecca's parents were part of a spiritual group. They co-authored a book called *Seeking the Light Within You* and went around the country running seminars. It took Mary a while to realise this was a kind of new-age Christianity. She didn't know Rebecca's take on it all, and couldn't bring herself to ask. Rebecca's mum had referred to her daughter as a very special being. She has access to things, and has a very old and profound soul, she'd said. Hearing this, Mary had thought to herself, cruelly, people think what they want about her because she's so beautiful.

Rebecca did move away at the end of the following year to study fine art at university. Her parents decided that, with their daughter gone and them being away for so much of the year, it was a good time to make a move themselves. They bought a house in the mountains in the south. Rebecca and Mary kept in touch, sometimes talking on the phone, sometimes sending emails and sometimes letters. Rebecca had a new boyfriend who was quite a bit older than Jack. She said, I didn't realise how much of a baby Jack had been. A year or so into the course, however, she phoned to say she was dropping out and moving into her parents' new place. Mary had noticed that references to spirituality were becoming increasingly prevalent in Rebecca's conversation and now Mary was really beginning to wonder what she wanted from this friendship. It was becoming difficult, she thought to herself, to get through to her friend in any real way. When Mary saw Jack at the café on the corner she realised any ill feeling she'd once had towards him had evaporated. She'd missed him. As he circumspectly said hello she resolved to act as though nothing had ever changed between them.

Rebecca travelled around the country with her parents and then went over to Europe and the US with them. From New Mexico, she sent Mary an A4 envelope filled with blown-up black-and-white photographs from her travels. There were photographs of stone doorways and bridges, and the rocky desert. By then, their correspondence had become sparse, so Mary didn't know what to make of this gesture. She thought to herself that Rebecca really has no excuse to still be looking at the world so naively, with such pretty eyes. Between two of the photos Mary found a small note with a dried flower taped onto the upper right-hand corner. The note read, 'Dear Mary. You have the power of clear vision and foresight in every part of your life. The blindfolds are removed. You grasp the cause-and-effect relationship that governs all reality. Your choices and actions are motivated by the ultimate result, not momentary illusions. You see more through your eyes; you receive more than through your mind's eye; you feel more through your intuition. Love, Rebecca'. On the back there was a pencil sketch of a woman with her face left blank beneath what appeared to be a wave and a copy of the dried flower that had been taped to the other side. Mary scrunched the note up. Rebecca must have copied this out from somewhere. It had nothing to do with her, she thought, this was Rebecca speaking to a god, or a god speaking to Rebecca.

Mary told Jack about the note. He said Rebecca had sent him a long email saying that he was beautiful and that she forgave him. In the email, she'd then said, I know you could never do this, but please forgive me too. I failed you, she'd written. She'd told him she'd met someone in Sante Fe and had decided she was going to stay there and live with him. He's magical like you are, she wrote. She'd attached a few photographs of her and her new boyfriend, and what was presumably their house and dog. The man looked like he was in his forties but it was hard to tell due to the size of his beard. This was a month ago, Jack said, and I haven't replied. I don't think I will, he said. Mary decided that if she were to write to Rebecca she wouldn't mention the packet of photographs and the note.

Several years later, Mary found Rebecca on Facebook and sent her a friend request. A month went by without Rebecca accepting the request, so Mary sent her a message saying she often thought of their friendship, that she deeply regretted not having stayed in touch. By the following morning, Rebecca had replied to say that she too wished she'd written more often. She was still in Sante Fe, where she lived with Malcolm and their two children in an old barn. They had a market garden. You would love it, she said, we're very self-sufficient. Mary pictured Rebecca in a floppy hat and pair of overalls that had been worn soft, along with her two children, their faces blurred, gathering up silverbeet, carrots and squash. Mary lived within the ecstasy of having heard back from Rebecca and the idea of their friendship being rekindled for a week before she could make herself write again. You have children, she wrote, how old are they, what are their names? But then a month went by and then another and Rebecca still hadn't replied a second time. Mary thought to herself that she ought to try again, that she would know what to say this time but by then, regretfully, she could no longer find within herself whatever it was that had been stirred by their brief correspondence.

MARY JEAN CHAN
FROM ARS POETICA

Mary Jean Chan is a Hong Kong-Chinese poet, lecturer, editor and critic. Their first poetry collection *Flèche* won the 2019 Costa Book Award for Poetry and was shortlisted in 2020 for the International Dylan Thomas Prize, the John Pollard Foundation International Poetry Prize and the Seamus Heaney Centre First Collection Poetry Prize. In 2021, *Flèche* was a Lambda Literary Award Finalist. Chan's second collection, *Bright Fear*, is forthcoming from Faber in 2023. Chan recently co-edited *100 Queer Poems* with Andrew McMillan. Chan is Senior Lecturer in Creative Writing (Poetry) at Oxford Brookes University and lives in Oxford.

I

When I was young, I realised my body
was something to be held back or kept
in its place, so I have mastered the art
of observation, how to watch faces for
a frown or grimace: signs of weather.
Once, a teacher came up to me in the
school playground and asked me if I
had any feelings. Your expression is
blank, she added. What could I say?
I knew how to dim any spark within.
Years later, I left home for the poem:
inscrutable house, constructed space,
blue room, how the poets have named
a heaven in which lonely meanings sit
companionably beside lonely children.

II
after Marie Howe

The novel feels like a springer spaniel running off-
leash the poem a warm basket it returns to always

As a teenager I learnt to minimize myself whenever
my mother's face transformed into a furious sunset

What does it feel like to not have to hide things like
a small splinter of sadness or an even smaller need?

I work too well with constraints so I cannot enjoy
the sheer amount of space a prose writer deserves

My therapist says it has to do with my relationship
to freedom something I find just as trying as prose

I want my reader to understand my protagonist and
their feelings without my having to describe them in

detail the way a poet I adore once wrote about her
brother a gate and a cheese and mustard sandwich

I accept that I can't comprehend the size or shape or
texture of the gate but I knew the shade of her grief

III

at twenty, you were as far   away from poetry
as you now are   from the sea
a man once   asked you where
you found grace   you told him in a poem

for years you thought   touch was the tap
running   your fingers braiding
the soft water   or the shower spilling
incandescently   over a shamed torso

at an airport in Texas   a barista playfully asked
if you were a professional   tennis player
praising your shoulders   you were
in transit to attend   a slam poetry contest

yet you felt seen somehow so you cleaved to that
small identity   all afternoon
comforted you had a place in that brutal country
that summer   you returned home

as yourself   then left once more
months later   clutching a slim book
of poems close on the long   flight to New York
each word a warm hand   to keep you

from the edge of things   each line a hum
to bring back   the hallelujah

IV

They wrote: NONFICTION, then saved it
in a folder titled FICTION, then saved it
in a folder titled POETRY. This felt true.

KATHARINA VOLCKMER
FRITZ

Katharina Volckmer was born in Germany in 1987. She now lives in London where she works for a literary agency. *The Appointment*, her first novel, was published by Fitzcarraldo Editions in 2020.

THAT'S WHERE I FOUND HIM, my mother said. That's where he must have collapsed. Lying on his side, that's how he met his inevitable fate. I laughed when my mother told me about this. There was something funny about picturing Fritz and his unshapely body in front of something as banal as a fridge. And even if he had become skinny towards the end of his life, his body strained by several unnamed illnesses, I'm sure that he was still ugly. His eyes too far away from each other to look into them without unease, his head too small, his belly reminiscent of a dysfunctional udder. Fritz had always been strangely effeminate but without knowing what to do with his female charms. Or maybe he was afraid of showing them in front of my older brother. It's what made him lovely though, this absence of any forceful masculinity that allowed him to pride himself with a good personality instead. Someone who was grateful that you had let them into your house, who'd eat anything without complaint. Who was gentle. Maybe someone who didn't deserve to die in front of an electrical appliance.

There was no point in moving him, my mother interrupted. It was going to happen anyway, you would've known if you had spent more time at home. And there is nothing wrong with dying in front of a fridge, it's a good fridge, remember? We haven't had it for too long. Even Elvis died on the toilet and that hasn't done anything to damage his reputation. On the contrary, look at all the stupid men still dressing up in Elvis costumes, even your brother used to listen to his music. Death can dignify a place. Have you ever thought of the space a dead body takes up as opposed to a living one? A still heart never has to fight for the right dimensions because we all agree on what they should be. That's why we grant them without complaint. In a way there weren't many better places for him to rest his soul, unless you would have liked for him to be dragged into the garden? To die with his eyes on the heavens. But it's a pretty long way for a dying body to be dragged all the way from the kitchen to the back of the house. And Fritz never cared much for the garden, I don't think. He would of course come outside with us, but really only to please my mother who had great faith in that miserable piece of lawn. But Fritz knew as well as us that there was never enough sunshine to defeat the slugs and that my mother needed this illusion to cope with things. To pretend this was the life she wanted. She might well want to be found collapsed on her side there one day, to be finally free from my brother and his childish demands. But she is right, it wouldn't have suited Fritz.

I don't dare to ask how long he would have been lying there before he was found listening to the pathetic hum of the fridge as it accompanied the failure of his organs. Going off one after the other, like the badly dressed losers in one of those soul-destroying game shows. One thing is to die alone but another is to die with such a stupid sound in the background. The opposite of a tragic violin – it's the sound we have become accustomed to as a signal that our food is safe. That we are acting in accordance with our expiry dates. And Fritz was lying there like that bag of those strange mixed vegetables we have never really believed in and finally found the momentum to chuck in the bin. Like one of the many objects we get through, Fritz had reached that dangerous threshold where our bodies finally lose their subjectivity. Where they become worldless in their pain and no longer carry a message others can read. He must have known that he was playing with fire when he was lingering outside the fridge that day.

I reckon it's what he wanted, my mother objects. He was often a bit pathetic and maybe this was just his way to go. For a moment I was worried that she would go to one of her darker places again and tell me that it didn't matter. That sooner or later the earth will be consumed by the sun. That the sun would one day become huge and swallow us. That all stars are going to die or are dead already and that not even the sun is special. But somehow my mother found the energy to stay focused on being alive. And maybe Fritz was relived to hear nothing but the strange silence emanating from the fridge, a somewhat milder version of dying next to the hoover. Remember that he was very partial to food. It's probably fair to say that he was fat before disease struck. I say disease but I don't know for sure what ailed him, I never really understood what it is that makes others die. Unless it's something drastic like an accident, something with a lot of blood or one of those dramatic conditions some people can't seem to get enough of. But Fritz was always rather private about his body, as if he knew that he would forever be locked into it. That his own body was his darkest cave and not just because he had never received much credit for the physical aspects of his existence. He had probably felt like a rather undesirable household member. Not unlike a younger sibling next to my beautiful brother. Like all younger siblings he would have known that our famous advantages are paid for by years of feeling small. Years of weakness as a biological fact that rendered our parents' excess of love nothing but an instinctual compensation, partly triggered by the guilt they felt over our lack of presence in their photo albums. My older brother has three entire volumes to himself whereas my little face disappears after a few pages at a ridiculous age – hardly bigger than the neighbour's cat and without teeth. A size I would never have been able to outgrow again, even if there had been a father in this story.

Since when did you care so much about him anyway? My mother forgets that I have known her for as long as she's known me. Don't you dare. How was I supposed to know he had died like this? Your brother was here when we buried him. That's because brothers are always there when somebody needs to be buried. Because they don't ever leave. Their childhoods are eternal. But in my mother's eyes leaving is nothing but a flaw. A stain on your character. It's never an act of courage unless you have to flee from some desperate situation and even then. If you start running you become prey, remember? People like her would gladly have shot soldiers returning to their home countries after having been captured by the enemy. Like she would shoot us all for refusing to die on that imaginary field of honour that she calls family. Leaving is not an option because that's when others die alone in front of their fridges. And I curse myself for not having the conversation I wanted to have. The conversation we never have because I failed to outgrow my toothless mouth, because in her ears my words are still mindless blabbering. More saliva than words, nothing that she needs to pay too much attention to. But I want to tell her about the leaving that's going on in my life right now. The partner I have betrayed. The shattering of a romance she's never had to endure. I suddenly want to ask her who it is she thinks about in the bath but I can hear the television in the background now, her voice becoming even more abstract. Sometimes you just don't know which one of you is moving and which one is standing still.

At least he wasn't killed by that dog, it sounds like she is looking for an excuse now. Or maybe a dog is featuring on her screen, but I doubt the dog in question had any serious plans for what remained of Fritz's life. I doubt it would have risked taking a bite of that disease-ridden flesh. I trust that even a dog would have that much instinct left, but then I saw a dog swallow a hygiene product the other day and I reckon even Fritz had more appeal than a mix of bodily fluids dried on absorbent cellulose and some strange gel pearls. Or maybe the dog had felt like dying too. But I don't understand my mother because I always thought that it would be a blessing to be killed by an animal. It would be an honour, imagine being torn apart by a family of lions. I can't think of anything more majestic, it's only humans that scare me. And now fridges. Since when are you so deranged? I don't have an honest answer to that question, but I keep thinking about the old woman's dog now whose name I have forgotten. Soon you will forget my name too, my mother adds. Does that mean that you remember everything about me? Do you remember how I felt on my eighth birthday or the name of my first real friend? Of course, she doesn't. She will always claim the better end of our distance. That's also why she is allowed to keep the TV on during our conversations. And I wasn't there to open the door that day, to let in whoever had come to try and help poor Fritz. I have no claim on her memories. Babbling and toothless, I remain a strange shape filled with guilt and my mother's accusations.

At least you missed out on the smell. He really stank towards the end, you could hardly sit next to him. I can't help it, but I'm laughing again and this time I'm hysterical, imagining Fritz and my mother on the couch together, like certain types of fruit that rot faster in each other's company. I can hear her frowning, she hates it when she finds me funny. Death isn't pretty, especially not with someone like Fritz. He must have started dying a long time ago, you know, that tipping point when the rot becomes permanent, like stains multiplying beyond your control. It's like someone else is in charge of your body without making you feel less alone. But you didn't pity him? Of course, she did. You mean pity him enough to? And with what? Do you think I'd just pick up a stone in the garden and club him to death in his sleep? The image doesn't seem that outlandish to me, but I keep that to myself, after all I'm her deranged child. Of course not, you would never do such a thing. You wouldn't want a dying body to burst. In the end we would have found you both lying there, his rot spoiling your last embraces.

My mother thinks that I don't know. Or that I have forgotten because it happened at night, and I often struggle to distinguish life from my dreams. But she is mistaken. I remember how you hit him that day. Don't tell me you never hit anyone in your life. It happened outside your bedroom door. I don't remember exactly how old Fritz was, but old enough for it to look tragic. Old enough for him to fall over and be at least mildly traumatised. Your generation never talks about anything else. You only remember the people who didn't call you on your birthday. Fritz was fine. He knew why I had done it. And he deserved it? We all deserve our fate. And he had a good life with us, he was always comfortable. Except for when you beat him up? You're exaggerating, he needed to be taught. Ultimately, pain is all that we remember, those moments that make us physical. When we are nothing but our bodies. I've never heard him cry, so it can't have been that bad. At least I was always there for him, I didn't just leave. A fist in the face being preferable to a lonely heart. I'm sure she would tell me that it wasn't a fist but merely a flat hand. Almost a tender gesture. And for a moment I think that maybe she is right. Maybe

I would like to be there with her now even if that meant that she might ambush me from her bedroom with something that wasn't a fist. Maybe my head could have taken the insult that was always too heavy for the rest of me.

You probably think that's why he started seeing ghosts. I feel like she is eyeing my most delicate spots now. I never believed that he could actually see ghosts, it just seemed like a possibility at the time. Because I hit him? Because he was clearly dealing with something, and supernatural phenomena are often a reaction to pain. I don't want to use the word trauma again and open doors of further ridicule. So, you also see saucers and funny white things flying around? What makes you say that? There is no need to spell it out, we both know that I don't usually call when I'm happy. I once read that hearing our mothers' voices has an immediate calming effect. It lowers our heart rate and makes us feel protected, which means by now my brother should be calmer than a saint. Or maybe this magic only applies once you have gone away and become a traitor. Maybe it's a way for the guilty to feel forgiven and I should really be using these calls as my personal road to redemption. But then Fritz never left her. That's right. He was always there for me. Didn't waste his time getting in and out of silly relationships. If I had to describe him in one word, I'd say he was faithful. Not sure that's a concept you can relate to. I don't know how she does it or why these moments of total transparency make me feel like she only just stopped changing my nappies. Like I still haven't found a way to hide even my bare skin from her. Has she also worked out that pain killers make me happy whilst these situations make me feel like I'm not even capable of loving a mother? That these phone calls make me feel bored by myself until it occurs to me that she might hate them as much as I do. That she would love to give in to her eyes' desire and just watch her stupid programme about a zoo rather than listen to my unfinished life. That my brother isn't just childish and ill-tempered but a source of comfort in the face of her other ridiculous child. That she would never think about me in the bath. My pulse is definitely not what I would call calm, if anything there is rage on the horizon and I would scream if it wouldn't make me feel even more like a toddler others had lost faith in. A strange creature with sticky fingers and no personal qualities to inspire a sense of curiosity for their future.

That's why I'm telling you, it felt natural for him to end this way, her voice is getting tired. To not aim higher than a cold and not very clean kitchen floor. That's probably why my mother never bothered to mention it. Why she took no exception to his final moments. And until now I don't know whether he has actually been buried or whether my mother made use of my brother's lack of sentiment and just went for cheap solution. Something you get away with in the countryside. I don't know whether there is any point in further stretching my bank balance by sending belated flowers. And so, I try not to find anything sinister in the way we laughed about the incident. I try to console myself by thinking that we don't even know what laughter is, something that we seem to share with rats and monkeys. A space we turn to when we have exhausted all other emotions. Laughter is the absence of my bad tears. When I throw myself into the unknowable hoping I will come out lighter at the other end, I sometimes laugh until my skin is filled with blood. Until I have found the only thing that is good when it's contagious. Making people laugh is harder than giving them pleasure but Fritz didn't care about any of this, I don't think he even knew how to laugh, and it wouldn't have done much for his unfortunate features. And he doesn't need it anymore, the laughter is for us, those he left behind. It's for us to share in between those strange silences when we realise that Death spent all those years hiding behind our fridge. Humming along to the decay of our groceries.

KATE MIDDLETON
TELEVISION POEMS

Kate Middleton is an Australian writer. She is the author of the poetry collections *Fire Season*, which was awarded the Western Australian Premier's Award for Poetry in 2009; *Ephemeral Waters*, shortlisted for the New South Wales Premier's Literary Award in 2014; and, most recently, *Passage*. From 2011–2012 she was the inaugural Sydney City Poet.

I

at last they put the poet on TV, the one they always
had to label: *spinster, recluse,* or else just *too intense*:

in her corset and her petticoats, we see her burrowing
to find her own blood, the monthly malady that starts

within, and when she throws herself into the most
dramatic wail, declares her pain in the greatest

ostentation, two taboos arise as once, against which
there is no inoculation: a poet, already a near-fatal

flaw, and, on TV, a wilfully unmarriageable woman:
it thrills me this mess of being, and television can only

push it further, can only make the poet a goth rock star,
saucy, charismatic, living some life I hadn't known

I'd dreamed of: I never liked *The Cosby Show* – at least,
I never liked Bill Cosby, which was not prescience, just

a wish to be left alone: of course when I was nine, ten,
eleven, I watched when it was on, and because I was

that age, I felt what Rudy felt: the only episodes
that stay with me these decades on are the ones about

the women, Clair's crash diet, losing weight to fit
a dress, a past, a disordered dream, or, most, when

Rudy menstruates at last, the last child's menarche,
and is embarrassed by the fuss: as I watched, I thought

I wanted it, the blood, the fuss, but I was also, myself,
humiliated by Dr Huxtable, his nosing over it, around,

his teasing Rudy, which played as one more dad joke,
not the symptom that I now suppose it was, even then:

when I did bleed, some months later, I found that same
humiliation, the conversation I'd rehearsed, how to tell

my mother I was somehow now more grown, a mush
of words I could not say: instead I tried to hide it: and

when I watch Emily dig up layer upon layer of white
cotton until she confirms the coming mess at last I see it

performed, the real response I feel each time: I was
listening to fans talk about the *Liars*, remembered

the way dialogue could ring true – *You are giving me
cramps* – and how audacity could be squelched, again,

with malicious voyeurism: and now, in youth, at least,
on screen, at least, the Amherst poet refuses to be

squelched, converses with the hallucinatory bee,
with Death, dares spectacle and hunger, dares

to strip the many layers back, dares deny at least
a moment that some rule will be laid down upon her

head, and she'll pay for such audacity with a sanitised
reputation, her words themselves subversive, any

other shape to her life storied into sheer seclusion, or
else those *wild nights* imagined for a new demographic:

I can only hope they'll appreciate her ribbons, her
bread, her pencil stubs, her uncompromising wants,

her strong hands, her words, her full disclosure of the blood

II

when the soap star faced accusations...when the sitcom star
faced accusations...when the novelty star faced accusations...

some days it seems like all the reassuring hams of broadcast
have had their masks ripped off: and, yes, when it comes

to reporting the sex crimes of the once-were 'rich and famous'
it all resembles *Scooby Doo* more than *SVU* – at least so long

as tabloids print, reprint, their remorseless voided faces, skate
across the jagged nerves of victims: a facade falls and the
portrait

of Dorian Gray looms alarmingly ordinary: we used to watch
Hey Dad..! as a family (my mum liked Nudge) and I was delighted

when I found Walgett on the map: Walgett, a *real* place, not
a television place: I wanted to go there, like the day years later

we drove my cousins to Bonnie Doon, and they sang, as
you must now, or you must if you're Anglo, *We're goin'*

to Bonnie Doon, because what they wanted was not
the destination, but the journeying toward: my parents

sure that the joke of being from Walgett (this joke somehow
got laughs) was the best thing about Walgett: erasure: TV's

pathology: we never went: and in suburban Sydney

the sitcom architect turned sinister – hey, 'dad', *there's*

a real evil in these studio lots: hey, 'dad' is a mask too,
worthy of *Twin Peaks*: Twin Peaks, which is not a real place

name, but the town is real, the diner's real, the Douglas fir trees,
and Douglas fir tree scent, all real – : the question, 'Who killed

Laura Palmer?' posed midway through *Hey Dad..!*'s
run, but on another channel, the ads for it, the mystery,

lingering a decade before I watched: yet I watched it too,
unknowing: Laura's trauma played out on *Hey Dad..!*'s set,

not yet knowing what I saw, a daughter, later recast, now
re-emerging to break nostalgia's grip, reveal the sickness:

it's happening again: and when the stories broke, a long
parade of faces – again: reassuring as childhood: broken

as childhood: looking up the history, Walgett's our hope,
Walgett where waters converge: *Hey Dad..!* never mentioned,

of course, the Freedom Rides, the protest: that history has nothing
to add to the hapless white single-dad story, so I suppose

we should be grateful that at least Betty was played for laughs
and not for sex appeal: and that Laura Palmer, played for sex, was

at least shown cyanotic, swaddled in death, in plastic, wrapped
in all the damage we've endured

III

a cast changeover, not a second string, but mid-career, mid-
life, reshuffle: churn: or the reminder that we all gain

that second chin, or its equivalent, in time: season three,
safe in the realm of historical memory, but episode one

and my mother unsure of this new queen: she tells me
how much she liked Claire Foy, Foy's radiance, radiance

of Coronation, Annunciation, capturing a sense of something
lost in us by years: then episode two, the switch to Margaret,

scandalous, and episode three it's coal, collieries, slurry,
the need for stricter regulation, the bodies of how many

children – 116 – buried under the labour we still want
to give a working class, for which we'll lease new seams,

the labour we still heroise in images as our televisions blaze
out late into the night: then there it is: the vision of the mountain

sliding down itself, engulfing the classroom, engulfing
every notion of innocence, over so quickly yet unforgettable:

I look up the psychological studies, the lasting testimony,
reactions of the surviving children: the Pied Piper brought

the mountain down to them, and yet some escaped the Piper's
wrath (when the Piper is an earth hollowed out and then refilled,

his wrath is terrible and inexact): the children tell the aftermath,
the wish to disappear, retreat indoors, retreat to silent footsteps,

downcast looks, the sense that existing in view is just
a reminder to the parents of the lost of what is lost:

everything: and yet, *carry on*, there is a better world
to forge: when I write I'm aware that each phrase,

each opinion, alienates me from half the population,
my politics inescapably detectable – and television helps

to reinforce this rift: we can agree on Foy's radiance, but not
facts: still, by episode three, we have adjusted to this new vision,

coal a crisis replacing fog, smog: mid-career must be
a rough spot for a monarch too, sheen worn off and image

showing scuffs: and Aberfan, deluge of slurry, of collapsing
mountainside, of landscape inundated with black, blackening

despair: we watch the years tick past, *The Crown* a moving
image timeline, and the welling tear, the second welling tear,

a moment still, a moment beyond embattlement and politics,
a moment deep in self-doubt and self-reflection: who hasn't

thought what this queen says at some time: *I have known*
for some time that there is something wrong with me: some

time, all of the time, there is surely something wrong with each
of us: I have always cried too much, once got sent home

from school for excessive anguish, so surely there is something
wrong with me, to be so swept, ineluctably, into such feeling,

perhaps an early sign of future diagnosis, and the twice-tried
drawdown from the years of medication – lachrymose weeks,

months, and then the doctors stating, *well I guess the pills do
something*: now Olivia Colman is the New Becky, alongside

an age-lined barrage of New Beckys (Old Beckys only ever
glimpsed in memory, and *Becky* an Aristotelean recognition

of species through the filtering out of any particulars, arrival at
the essence) while the promise of the next generation comes

into view: meanwhile, Prince Andrew *stepping back*, this
from television too, disastrous interview, backlash, audience

primed to outrage, scripted into choice of villain, concentrating
discontent, and the pronouncement from the palace never quite

attuned to current feeling, as if such tempering is ever possible:
they, *we*, learn it all again: there is no commensuration

Notes

I

In *Dickinson* we see a young, queered, surreal-tinged Emily Dickinson and I love it. The episode of *The Cosby Show* in which Rudy gets her period is called 'The Infantry Has Landed (And They've Fallen off the Roof)'. All she wanted was for this occasion to pass invisibly, a sentiment that resonated with my own experience. Aria says, 'You're giving me cramps' in the the episode, 'She's No Angel', in season six of *Pretty Little Liars*. 'Wild nights' refers to not just a Dickinson poem, but also to the movie *Wild Nights with Emily*, a queer period rom-com telling of Dickinson's relationship with Sue Huntington Gilbert Dickinson.

II

The trial of *Hey Dad..!*'s Robert Hughes is just one in a spate of unmasked abuses. Alongside *Hey Dad..!* this poem references the cartoon *Scooby Doo* (and arguably echoes the use of the 'Scooby Doo Ending' suggested in *Wayne's World*), the series *Law and Order: SVU*, the Oscar Wilde novel *The Picture of Dorian Gray*, the film *The Castle* and the David Lynch show *Twin Peaks*. David Lynch's *Twin Peaks* is often cited for its surrealism; however, its too-real contemplation of the abuse hidden by the veneer of suburban life is what stays with me.

III

It's hard, being Kate Middleton and being uninterested in the royals. Sometimes the royals are thrust upon you. When *The Crown* started, I didn't know that I too would fall for it, but I did. And while I enjoy the politics and palace gossip of it, it's really the environmental episodes that have stayed with me – the London smog in season one, and Aberfan, in season three. The loss of so many children at Aberfan has been the subject of psychological study. 'New Becky' refers to the replacement of the original actress playing Becky in the show *Roseanne*. A friend said, 'I can't believe you called Olivia Coleman a New Becky.' I did.

STEPHANIE RADOK
UNDER THE BED

The only dream worth having is to dream that you will live
while you are alive, and die only when you are dead.

Arundhati Roy, *The End of Imagination*

The gardener digs in another time, without past or future,
beginning or end...As you walk in the garden you pass into this
time – the moment of entering can never be remembered.

Derek Jarman, *Modern Nature*

Stephanie Radok is a writer and artist living on Kaurna country. She worked as an art critic and editor with *Artlink, Artlink Indigenous* and *The Adelaide Review*. Her books *An Opening: Twelve Love Stories About Art* – which was longlisted for the inaugural Stella Prize – and *Becoming a Bird: Untold Stories About Art* were published by Wakefield Press. Her work is in the collections of the National Gallery of Victoria and the National Gallery of Australia.

TODAY I WATERED THE FRONT GARDEN BY HAND. Maybe not the most efficient method but efficiency has its limits. I decided to pick three long stalks of feverfew daisies growing near the nectarine tree as they had started to lie down. They have an intense and complex scent half-mint half-chrysanthemum. It is an insect-repelling herb.

I said to the dog, the garden is giving us flowers. And as I held them in front of me and walked towards the mirror in the front hall I was reminded of the artist Paula Modersohn-Becker who painted herself several times holding flowers in front of her.

It felt ceremonial and I found my camera, pushed the flowers into the front of my shirt and took a few photos. It was a kind of homage. Both to my mother, who loved to place flowers in vases, and to Modersohn-Becker, who died at thirty-one after childbirth, and was a friend of poet Rainer Maria Rilke after whom my father was named. It was for them too.

Rilke wrote a prose work dedicated to her called 'Requiem for a Friend' in which, in a translation by Stephen Mitchell, appear the words:

You had just one desire: a years-long work—
which was not finished, in spite of all your efforts.

If you are still here with me, if in this darkness
there is still some place where your spirit resonates
on the shallow sound-waves stirred up by my voice:
hear me; help me. We can so easily
slip back from what we have struggled to attain
abruptly, into a life we never wanted;
can find ourselves entangled, as in a dream,
and die there, without ever waking up.

Ah Rilke and ah the work. The groping, the plans, the reality, and yet how to begin and how to go on. The what and the why and the who for and the how all rise up towards the solitary artist or writer asking them so many questions and providing so few answers. A years-long work.

There are the interruptions of domesticity, of what we tell ourselves, and what we make ourselves believe, especially for women who often like to give and make life better or at least good for those around them. Feminist icon Ann Newmarch often spoke of interrupted time as a mother and artist and that is, in some way, what Rilke is also describing, the dream of continuity versus the reality of daily life, and all its ways of breaking up the day. Before she died I asked Newmarch for the origin of the resonant quotation that she used in a print in 1975: 'We must risk unlearning all the things that have kept us alive for so long.' She told me that she could not remember.

The rosemary is full of blue flowers. The purple native hibiscus is flowering. The jade tree is covered in mounds of pale pink stars.

In the blue gum hanging over the back fence a koala, a rounded Buddha, a clot of grey in the sky, sits and watches, eats and drops brown scats. On a wet day its ears are like the soft grey-white fluffy heads of dandelions.

Even though some yellow leaves are still hanging on trees and vines new buds are already forming everywhere. The glory vine has delicate green buds starting out of dry sticks. This means if I prune it now it will drip clear sap like tears for a day or two. So, the sap is rising, there is no real downtime in the lives of the trees and other plants but constant movement from one state to another.

The garden is also full of soursobs, bright green and acid

yellow. You are supposed to wait until they are flowering before pulling them up and the hope is that their brown bulbs will come out at the same time, which they do, sometimes. The yellow jasmine is also flowering while the buds on the pink one are increasing in size every day.

The snowdrops are starting to come out. I used to think they were the only flowers in the world with green on them and that they had no perfume but when you pick their white bells and bring them inside after a while you notice their scent which is like a liqueur, fragrant and volatile. And the japonica is out, orange and spiky.

On the way to the playground at the top of the street, where the dog and I go almost every day to play ball, there is a small eucalyptus on which hang about fifty chrysalises made from pieces of torn leaves placed together to form what look like tiny pine cones. Like the koalas they are camouflaged. They must have been made by caterpillars. Some of them look quite dry while others are fresher. They have an Egyptian or Mesopotamian quality to them and also a Christmas bauble feeling. One day soon I am going to bring a small branch home so that I can find out what creature they are housing. If I had an old aquarium I would put them in there but might find a vase to hang it in instead.

And I realise that I am something like one of these invisible creatures and have built a layered home around myself of books, a garden, art, and perhaps most valuable of all – pieces of paper on which vital words wait to be followed through or placed with others.

Drops of water hang in all the trees and bushes, evenly spaced on the crabapple tree branches, in nets on the casuarina, and as shining lights all over the lacy fennel and daisy leaves. Writing is like embroidering with threads taken from the world and from thought, beads of insight, fragments of flowers and seeds, as well as lots of dust that has accumulated and holds time in its imperceptible motion.

In the middle of the night, around four a.m., sometimes/ often/but not always, a bird sings a four-note song at intervals. It doesn't wake me up but when I lie there I hear it and imagine it is letting all the other birds and the rest of us know that all is well. Morning is coming.

What shall I do? How often do I open my hands and hold them out to the night? Calling the stars to witness. As a gesture in solitude, it has some drama...and could even be called Rilkean.

A years-long work. There is a kind of archive fever around me – stumbling over piles of my own past, notes, images, objects, I also encounter the pasts of others, people all over the world, family and friends, streaming away in all directions. When I leave the house and go to the market I see stories piled up in every face, every encounter, every piece of clothing, every smile. The idea of treasures, of gifts for the future, folded inside the archives, is, for me, one large reason they exist. Yet getting them out needs more than a systematic mind or indeed a system because an organic archive leaks away in all directions.

I sit on my bedroom floor surrounded by notebooks of every conceivable size, colour and shape. There is no regimentation in this life, even though it includes making notes and writing – there is no tidy progress, no inventory, no order! Damn. Just a great volume of pages scrawled, written, scribbled. Lists for self-improvement, complaints, dreams (a lot of dreams), visions (quite a few), appointments, plans, events, joy, manifestos, copied out passages from books, anger, drawings, misery, shopping lists and accounts, delight, and here and there a flight of writing, and sometimes a poem or something like one lying on its side, half-dead, half-alive, wondering if it will be pulled out and resuscitated or left there.

Like all artists, writers are self-appointed and must have both very thick and very thin skins: thick to withstand indifference, thin to make their observations, and to find the fine edges of meaning in their languages.

Writing is or can be a consoling voice whether you are the writer or the reader. It can wrap you in a warm hug of solace, not always so much the content as the rhythm, the mood and the sense of a world with a form. Then there is sometimes the feeling of being transported to another place, another level of existence, the home of heightened and intensified sensations.

So, here all around me, are multiple notebooks filled with too much embarrassing nonsense and self-revelation to be safe. No one must ever see these books. It is imperative for me to stay alive long enough to find and destroy them all.

But first I must identify the treasure in them as those few words may keep me or someone else alive. A sense of duty enters here. In some ways it is a defiant echo of myself as a child. When I learned something off by heart I imagined saving lives by knowing those words. We will murder you all, unless someone knows this poem or song, they would say. I can do it, I would pipe up. Memory as power.

Every now and then a shelf of notebooks that I had forgotten turns up to frighten me. And then I appreciate the common sense of religious rituals that, as a side effect, include cleaning the entire house. I particularly like the description of the Jewish one of ridding the house of bread before Passover that Claudia Roden describes in her Jewish cookbook. Thus religion can improve hygiene, and maybe this is one key to its endurance, as well as a way to remove secrets and trails. But how likely is it, really, that all secrets can be removed? Don't we all need them to give our lives depth?

There are notebooks stacked in an old desk, some in a cupboard, piles in a box or two. They are without labels though some have dates written on their covers from former attempts to impose order and some have bookmarks or dogears marking notable moments. They are museums, libraries, suitcases, vitrines, bookshelves, archives, wasteplaces and storerooms. When I hear about someone using the same type of notebook all their life and clearly dating and filing them as if their existence was a neat shelf of bound journals in a library I feel sad. My notebooks lack such a steady rhythm. Such regularity sounds suffocating anyway – the appeal of the random, the accidental, the chance, the unpredictable, except in the case of breakfast, is surely essential and needed for a life to be alive. Patterns can be found later.

The earliest notebooks are tiny, lined booklets, though there are a few unusual heritage notebooks, resuscitated vintage items discovered in op shops. These are followed by exercise books and something relentless starts to happen here as writing becomes as rewarding, in some way, as living, and must be fulfilled, not for posterity, not as a public work to be polished and published or submitted for publication but as release, as pleasure, as necessity.

There are a few volumes from a bookbinding class I took in

Canberra, amazing old-fashioned real proper thick hardcover books – one blue, one red, one grey, stitched, stiff, stout and strong – they will be quite hard to burn but I will give it a go.

Then there are the patterned books that a designer has composed to give life a bit of style and colour. There are books of every description imaginable, cheap and ordinary, spiral-bound, stapled, and plain as so often are my hand-written words, though rampant in their scale. Yet sometimes mesmerising, hypnotic, holding even in the thickness or thinness of their inked letters a flavour of the time and the mood they record. While I did once mix my own ink from red and blue to make purple ink in my Baudelaire days of using a fountain pen, mostly it is black or blue that marks the pages, and I recall the scent of some biros to be really spicy and inky. There are at least a dozen red and black Chinese notebooks (from both during and after Mao). Then there are the Moleskines, legendary notebooks, beloved of Bruce Chatwin and others. Shiny or matte black, brown paper plain or red lizard skin, whether handsome or restrained in colouring they remain anonymous as they have no markers on the outside. Here and there is the book too good-looking to use. The notebook destined for emptiness, its beauty holding off revelation, confidences or simple documentation.

Will I ever be able to mine the notebooks and then destroy them? Why don't I just throw them all away? Can I relive the past? Is it safer, quieter, eternal? What is it that makes me keep them and occasionally pull one out to try to recreate something with it? Regret, sadness, longing, ambition? In a way it is like walking in a mysterious museum with always more rooms, dim galleries, doorways receding into infinity, glass vitrines with fruit and seeds from ancient tombs, fragments of china and glass beads from lost civilisations. Is it a huge monument to a pathological self-regard or a simple resource, an old jewellery box, a place of unthreaded moments?

A palace of memory. They are a garden too, old, rather overgrown, neglected, abandoned, wild. And must stay wild. The unpacking must be done privately. Secrecy and tenderness are the passwords/bywords. And the people within are often like closed books, sometimes they open a little. Some people go out, some go in and don't appear again.

The notebooks hang over me like an albatross might, if I had one. All the unspoken words piled up, heaped like earth, compost, weeds, leaves, refuse or fertiliser.

Really I have a deep inclination to just crawl under the bed and hide. I seek oblivion and ecstasy, silence and invisibility. Under the bed there is not much room, it is full of rolled up paintings but I think I can fit. And that is where you might find me, under the bed with the paintings, with my paintings.

Yet in this early spring the sky glows intensely just before dark and I must either watch from a window or go out and stand in the garden breathing and holding the light, letting it colour me in. Tonight I see a new moon and a star representing, to my fond imagining, a woman and her dog. Standing, staying, shining.

Finding the treasure. A years-long work.

NOËLLE JANACZEWSKA
STILL LIFE WITH CHEESE

Noëlle Janaczewska is a playwright, poet and essayist. She is the author of *The Book of Thistles* – part environmental history, part poetry, part memoir – and the collection *Scratchland*, both published by UWAP. She is the recipient of multiple awards, fellowships and residencies, including the 2020 New South Wales Premier's Digital History Prize and a Windham-Campbell Prize from Yale for her body of work as a dramatist. Noëlle's most recent productions include *Mrs C Private Detective* (ABC Radio National, 2022) and *The End of Winter* (Siren Theatre Company, Sydney, 2022).

Overleaf
Clara Peeters, *Still Life with Cheeses, Artichoke, and Cherries* 1625
oil on wood
courtesy Los Angeles County
Museum of Art www.lacma.org

I DON'T KNOW MUCH ABOUT CHEESE, but I know what I like. Crumbly wensleydale. Comté. Provolone. Taleggio. Stilton. Cumin-studded leyden. Sage derby...

I'm taking in the geometry of a cheese showcase in Sydney. The arrangement of semicircles, triangles, squares and rectangles. Blocks from here, and from there – France, Italy, England, the Netherlands. I have a modest and much treasured collection of old geography textbooks and atlases, and as I regard this cheesy cornucopia I'm concocting one of their charts. Printed with an economy of colour and detail: *The Global Travels of Cheese.*

Tasmanian brie, cheese infused with lemon myrtle, Persian feta, quark from Germany, extra creamy, extra bitey, salt reduced, vegan. The sunny profile of double gloucester. Port-salut from Brittany. Hard pressed, stretched curd and strong cheese. Yellow discs, red-waxed spheres, parsley-speckled, cranberry-layered, washed rind, cave-aged, smoked, soft, blue, goat – not too keen on goat to be honest.

Neighbourhood supermarkets – be they in Sydney, in Amsterdam, or anywhere else for that matter – reveal not only what the locals are eating, but a whole subtext of culinary attitudes. They're my first port of call in a foreign city. So it's after investigating the Albert Heijn supermarket on Leidsestraat that I walk to another place I always go whenever I'm in Amsterdam: the Rijksmuseum. Through streets that smell of spilt beer, dope, and that canal-damp common to water cities the world over. Visitors rush to Rembrandt. The gift shop is selling bars of soap disguised as emmental or its budget lookalike, maasdam. But there's less cheese on the walls than I remember, and as I gaze at the sole 'cheese painting' on show I wonder if the abundance of my previous trips is something I've imagined.

Tiers of cheese are centre stage in many still lifes from the opening decades of the seventeenth century. Hefty half-wheels anchor Floris Claesz van Dijck's 1615 painting. Ditto paintings by Floris van Schooten and Clara Peeters that I've seen reproduced online and in print. Still lifes from this period typically depict domestic fare, the components of a simple meal, and are known as *ontbijtje* (breakfast pieces). Bread and cheese, maybe an artichoke or a herring, a tankard of beer. All very egalitarian.

After slim pickings on the cheese-in-art front I turn my attention to the artistry of Amsterdam's cheese shops with their close-packed shelves and suggested 'threesomes' (buy three get a discount). From an array of cheeses labelled 'farmhouse lunch' I select a quarter moon of brandnetelkaas, its pale face freckled with foraged nettle.

Standing here surrounded by cheese of all hues and provenance I'm reminded of that famous passage in *Le Ventre de Paris* (*The Belly of Paris*) by one of my favourite writers, Émile Zola. The novel is set in Les Halles, the central food market that was demolished in 1971 and replaced by a Westfield mall. About three-quarters of the way into the book Zola orchestrates the contents of Madame Lecoeur's cheese storeroom into an olfactory symphony.

It was the camembert they could smell. This cheese, with its gamy odour, had overpowered the milder smells of the marolles and the limbourg; its power was remarkable. Every now and then, however, a slight whiff, a flute-like note, came from the parmesan, while the bries came into play with their soft, musty smell, the gentle sound, so to speak, of a damp tambourine. The livarot launched into an overwhelming reprise, and the gérome kept up the symphony with a sustained high note.

Cheese is a cheese is a cheese.

The story goes like this. Cheese is a fermented product created from milk, salt, rennet and a cast of powerful – albeit invisible to us – microbes. With a type such as emmental, cheesewrights depend on a particular bacteria to consume the lactic acid and release carbon dioxide. Carbon dioxide bubbles are trapped in the curd and form 'eyes'. Once upon a time these organisms were introduced to the milk via splinters of hay or grass. Over the past half-century however, as cheesemaking became a more hygiene-regulated procedure, makers found their emmental was failing to produce eyes. This resulted in what's called a blind cheese, and emmental minus its signature holes is considered substandard.

Cheesewrights. Playwrights. I like those 'wright' words for makers and builders of things. Turn out cheese. Shape a play. Overheard conversations on the bus. Snapshots of people briefly encountered. As a playwright I source my ingredients from routine as well as random places. A while ago I accompanied a friend to an upmarket delicatessen in an upmarket district of London. When I asked the specialist cheesemonger, a lanky thirty-something with hair the colour of gravel, if they had any sage derby, he responded with a barely suppressed shudder. 'It's flavour-added and we don't stock that kind of cheese,' he said, as he ushered us out of the shop. Was he worried the mere mention of a 'flavour-added' cheese would pollute his snooty business? Who knows, but one day I'll put him in a script and get my revenge.

A poet's hope: to be,
like some valley cheese,
local, but prized elsewhere.

W.H. Auden had been living in the Big Apple for years when he penned that stanza. Nevertheless I reckon the 'valley cheese' he had in mind was most likely an English one.

I like the English classics: sage derby, lancashire, stilton, wensleydale. Regional recipes now spread far and wide, e.g. my fridge contains a pack of sage derby from Victoria's Gippsland. It's a smooth, pleasantly fragrant cheese, goes well with baked pears and celeriac, but it doesn't taste like the sage derbies of my English growing-up. Is that the different terroir? Or is it more about the nature of memory? (Can you use 'terroir' for cheese, or does it only apply to wine?)

'That's it – cheese! We'll go somewhere where there's cheese!' exclaims inventor Wallace in the animated short *A Grand Day Out*. And off they rocket to the moon, because as everyone knows, the moon is made of cheese. Whenever I buy wensleydale, which I do quite often, I have that line echoing in my head. Cheese features regularly in the Wallace and Gromit films; the cartoon characters' enthusiasm for wensleydale is credited with boosting sales of the Yorkshire speciality. And they're in good company. T.S. Eliot dubbed wensleydale the Mozart of cheese. For George Orwell it was outclassed only by stilton.

Although the label 'Golden Age' is enough to make any dish sound appetising, Dutch cooking is hardly one of the world's celebrated cuisines. One food writer lamented at length the terrible influence of the potato on the nation's culinary arts. So what brought about such food-focused visual art?

According to nineteenth-century French critic Alfred Michiels, it was the weather. A cold, ungenial climate that sent people scurrying indoors fostered the development of Dutch and Flemish still-life painting.

Art historian Julie Berger Hochstrasser gives a rather different explanation:

The genesis of still-life painting as an independent genre coincides in time and place with a key period in the birth of consumer society. In the seventeenth century, the United Provinces of the Netherlands achieved a position of primacy in global trade that brought unprecedented wealth to Holland.

In the hierarchy of painterly subject matter, biblical and mythological scenes were the most prestigious. Until still lifes demoted the Holy Family and replaced them with flowers, fish, and yes, cheese. A mainstay of the agrarian economy and a food that carried no obvious religious meaning.

Was there cheese at the Last Supper? And if there was, what kind of cheese did Jesus and his disciples enjoy? Labneh? Haloumi? Ewes'-milk feta? Maybe Turkish lor – a cheese made from leftover whey that pairs brilliantly with sour cherry jam.

Which brings me to my next question: Who invented cheese?

Without refrigeration milk soon spoils. At some point

millennia ago herders worked out how to convert their milk into cheese, a more stable source of nourishment. The cheeses that evolved in various locations – the Mediterranean, the Middle East, Europe and elsewhere – were shaped by the physical and cultural characteristics of their particular environments.

Adding flavourings to cheese is a very old practice. Herbs, peppercorns, spices, even weeds. Sage derby is a semi-hard English cheese with a subtle, slightly grassy flavour. Its green marbling comes from sage, sometimes supplemented with spinach juice, which is added to the curds during the making (rather than the ageing) process. First produced in the seventeenth century and initially only for festive occasions, sage was thought to aid digestion and temper anxiety. There are detailed instructions for making it in the gloriously titled 1728 tome *The Country Housewife and Lady's Director in the Management of a House, and the Delights and Profits of a Farm.*

From farmhouse to factory, craft to commerce. On dairy holdings men took care of the outside tasks while wives did the inside labour – chores, children, cheese-making. Knowledge passed down the generations, from mothers to daughters... until around the middle of the nineteenth century when the profit potential of cheese became apparent. Large-scale manufacturing began, and surprise, surprise, it became a male-dominated industry.

Masters of the Golden Age – does that collective noun include women? It should because there were a number of successful female artists in the Low Countries during the seventeenth and early eighteenth centuries. Judith Leyster, Maria Sibylla Merian, Rachel Ruysch, Maria van Oosterwijck, Clara Peeters – and others. Of those painters only Clara Peeters did cheese. As far as I know. *Still Life with Cheeses, Artichoke, and Cherries* from 1625 is my favourite. As well as cheese (and biscuits), artichokes were one of Clara Peeters's trademarks. So too, reflected self-portraits that you need a magnifying glass to spot.

Biographical information about Clara Peeters is scarce and somewhat speculative. She may have been born in Antwerp around 1594. Or not. Probably was. In any case, she was one of the pioneers of still-life painting in the Netherlands. In the meticulous detail of her cheeses, I see landscapes. Knife cuts; cracks. A plugged hole left by the taster's scoop. Darkening edges; tiny blooms of mould. Dutch engineers taming the North Sea and draining the land to turn a soggy backwater into a dairy powerhouse.

It would be easy to assume no one went hungry during this period of plenty. Not so. Substantial sections of the population were living in poverty with a monotonous and wholly inadequate diet.

Twentieth-century artists took a more oblique approach to the art-reality nexus than their predecessors. René Magritte put a framed picture of a wedge of brie under a glass dome and declared: *Ceci est un morceau de fromage* – 'this is a piece of cheese'. Pop artist Roy Lichtenstein adopted Swiss cheese as a recurrent motif. *Cheese Head* was a billboard poster created for a 1978 exhibition, and *Jobs... Not Cheese!* was a critique of Ronald Reagan's apocryphal 'let them eat cheese' statement. Reagan enacted a program to offload the government's surplus – and frequently mouldy – processed cheese onto welfare recipients.

Imagine your cheese grater almost two metres high – that's

Mona Hatoum's *Grater Divide* from 2002. With the change of scale, an everyday kitchen utensil is recast as something alien. Something sharp and sinister. Then there's Rodin's *The Kiss* rendered life-size in cheddar. Yes, really. It was made for a 2015 competition aimed at raising money for UK museums and galleries.

Cheese is a cheese is a cheese.

And once upon a time it was a mysterious substance. An untrustworthy product, the preserve of dairymaids and cheese-wives, i.e. uneducated women. An unsettling entity within which lurked the stuff of nightmares. So went the thinking of the Middle Ages and Renaissance. In *The Cheese and the Worms* Carlo Ginzburg digs deep into archival records to give us the worldview of a sixteenth-century miller who believed that the cosmos and its inhabitants were created from rotting cheese. All was chaos 'thrashed by the water of the sea like foam, and it curdled like a cheese, from which later great multitudes of worms were born'.

Is cheese alive? (Short answer: yes.) An odd question to ask now perhaps, but back then it would have been easy to believe that there was something animate, something otherworldly about cheese. A notion that persisted well into the seventeenth century when polymath Margaret Cavendish wrote in her *Observations Upon Experimental Philosophy* that 'such insects, as Maggots, and several sorts of Worms and Flies, and the like, which have no Generator of their own kind, but are bred out of Cheese, Earth and Dung, &c.'

Cheese disappeared after about 1625. Not from the Dutch pantry, but from still-life paintings. Displaced by goods gathered from further afield. Porcelain and pineapples. Tropical birds. Items unfamiliar to European eyes. In 1596 Dutch ships reached the Indonesian archipelago. Shortly thereafter they went west to the Americas. The elaborate, over-the-top still lifes from the later seventeenth century are full of the fruits of empire, and one way to read these paintings is as a kind of map.

From homegrown comforts to the realities of colonialism. The spectre of slavery hovers over this bounty.

Julie Berger Hochstrasser again:

Just what and how much did the buyers, owners, and viewers of these paintings in their time know of the true stories of the acquisition of these many commodities assembled, mute but splendid, in Dutch still life?

A grape withers and falls from the bunch. A caterpillar munches a leaf. Pockmarks appear on a hunk of edam. Early interpretations of still lifes posited them as warnings. The moral danger of luxury or gluttonous excess. Later commentators spotlight the economic backstory. These lavish spreads celebrate independence and the newly proclaimed Dutch Republic's material prosperity.

Truth is, there are many possible meanings.

When gorgonzola became Google Scholar it wasn't the only cheese to flip. Gouda became Buddha. Word autocorrects hijack my typing and the resulting translations read like a Dada poem someone wearing a birdcage might have performed in Zürich circa 1918.

Google Scholar

Buddha

Important fonts (imported fontina)

Stand alone (stilton)

Cheese crackers

For a long time female artists were missing from histories of Dada. Or mentioned only as lovers and helpers. Hannah Höch, one of the few recognised by the movement, was dismissed in a male colleague's memoir-cum-chronology as a lightweight, the girl who provided the catering, 'Sandwiches, beer and coffee.' *Cut with the Kitchen Knife* is probably Hannah Höch's best known photomontage. So yes, put her in the kitchen shaving cheese – I'm picturing a creamy, raw-milk tilsit or maybe gruyère – then note the work's full title, *Cut with the Kitchen Knife Dada Through the Last Weimar Beer-Belly Cultural Epoch of Germany*, and we're no longer in the kitchen composing sandwiches. We're looking at a forceful, kaleidoscopic vision of German society.

Marcel Duchamp may have coined the term readymades, but he wasn't the first to reposition the materials of everyday life as art objects. A year before he devised his first readymade, Elsa von Freytag-Loringhoven a.k.a. the Baroness showed hers. And in 1917 when Duchamp submitted his now famous *Fountain*, she gave us *God*, a plumbing U-bend as sculpture. A big fuck you to the art establishment and to the powers that be.

Throw another question at Google: What's the most widely produced cheese?

Cheddar. At least thirteen countries churn out their own.

How about processed cheese – what's the deal there?

Kraft developed its processed cheddar in the United

States and launched it in Australia in 1925. Their 'cheese-like substance' had a lengthy shelf life and could be stored without refrigeration. The arrival of a local competitor, Maxam Cheese, three years later, sparked the ire of the Kraft Walker Company and a fiery and protracted legal battle ensued.

What art – if any – might be inspired by mass produced cheese? Kraft Singles instead of Andy Warhol's *Campbell's Soup Cans*? Or something agit-prop-y and satirical in the style of Barbara Kruger's slogans? 'Eat The Big Cheeses!' in Futura Bold?

A long time ago, I sat in a theatre with half a dozen other audience members, listened to an audioscape of industrial noise and watched a woman take an hour to peel an apple. I recall an untouched slab of cheese on a side table. I checked my watch. What would the performer do if I walked on stage and helped myself to a snack? Was it a plastic prop or the real article? Checked my watch again. Was the artist trying to say something about gendered labour? Capitalism? Original sin? Was it some sort of homage to Marina Abramović? Were the apple and cheese a reference to the verisimilitude of traditional still life? One positive thing I can say about the experience, is that instead of following the boringly predictable – but then fashionable – route and appearing naked, apple-woman remained fully clothed throughout.

Could the tart in Clara Peeters's still life with a tart be a cheesy one?

Cheese and onion pie.
Cauliflower cheese.
Fondue.

Börek.

Matar paneer.

Macaroni cheese.

Liptauer from Slovakia.

New York cheesecake.

Russian paskha.

New Zealand's famous – or infamous – cheese rolls.

Cookery books of the past were written for women who knew what was what. Their recipes hands-on, narrative rather than prescriptive.

I read somewhere – at least I think I did – the argument that still-life paintings have no narrative. They're purely description, the visual equivalent of literary exposition.

I have to disagree with that.

I love the chiaroscuro of those Dutch and Flemish canvases. I love their sensuality. When I look at them I can smell butter, nutmeg, a faint rasping of citrus. But most of all I love their drama. The table is set, food is offered, householders and guests partake and depart. The playwright in me conjures up an ensemble of players: the cooks and kitchen hands, the teenage servant girls who sweep up the crumbs, the provedores and market gardeners who supply the vegetables, the late-season plums, the cheese. Of course, the cheese. I concoct bios and dialogue, dream up scenarios that speak of intimate connections, of simmering tensions and treacherous acts. Mouth-wateringly beautiful in themselves, those still-life paintings are also trapdoors to the beguiling, candlelit universe of Jacobean theatre.

The Art Gallery of New South Wales has no still-life cheese on display and nothing by Clara Peeters, but they do have Maria van Oosterwijck's *Flowers and Grapes Hanging from a Ring*. It's apparently the earliest painting by a female artist in their collection.

I didn't know much about cheese, but in the course of researching this essay I've become a gleaner of thin-sliced facts and maybe-facts. From a Queensland dairy firm's plan to make a monster cheese for the 1905 Brisbane Show to the origin myth of camembert. From ancient, plant-derived coagulants to that perfect wensleydale savoured by a couple of spies in Graham Greene's *Our Man in Havana*.

Cheese is a cheese is a cheese.

And last month it was German walnut. My cheese of choice. This week it's a Dutch artisan gouda, dusky orange in colour, twenty-four months matured. I discovered it browsing the selection at that Sydney deli counter. Much as I want to try it however, at sixty-one dollars ninety-nine a kilo, I buy only a very small piece. I might grate it over baked zucchini with a pinch of mace, or over pasta instead of my usual grana padano, or...or I might just go home, watch trash TV, eat hot, bubbling gouda, glued to Polish rye bread with a dab of mustard, and sip a glass or two of carefully chosen mellow rioja.

Sources

Margaret Cavendish, *Observations Upon Experimental Philosophy*, A. Maxwell, 1666.

Andrew Dalby, *Cheese: A Global History*, Reaktion Books, 2009.

Carlo Ginzburg, *The Cheese and the Worms: The Cosmos of a Sixteenth-Century Miller*, translated by John and Anne Tedeschi, The Johns Hopkins University Press, 1980.

Julie Berger Hochstrasser, *Still Life and Trade in the Dutch Golden Age*, Yale University Press, 2007.

Paul S. Kindstedt, *Cheese and Culture: A History of Cheese and its Place in Western Civilization*, Chelsea Green Publishing, 2012.

Alfred Michiels, *Histoire de la Peinture Flamande et Hollandaise*, Librairie Ancienne et Moderne de A. Vandale, 1845–1848.

Simon Schama, *The Embarrassment of Riches*, Collins, 1987.

Émile Zola, *The Belly of Paris*, translated by Brian Nelson, Oxford University Press, 2007.

Acknowledgements

We respectfully acknowledge the Gadigal, Burramattagal and Cammeraygal peoples, the traditional owners of the lands where Giramondo's offices are located. We extend our respects to their ancestors and to all First Nations peoples and Elders.

HEAT Series 3 Number 5 has been prepared in collaboration with Ligare Book Printers, Avon Graphics, Ball & Doggett paper suppliers and Candida Stationery; we thank them for their support.

The Giramondo Publishing Company is grateful for the support of Western Sydney University in the implementation of its book publishing program.

Giramondo Publishing is assisted by the Australian Government through the Australia Council for the Arts.

HEAT Series 3
Editor Alexandra Christie
Designer Jenny Grigg
Typesetter Andrew Davies
Copyeditor Aleesha Paz
Marketing and Publicity Manager Kate Prendergast
Publishers Ivor Indyk and Evelyn Juers
Associate Publisher Nick Tapper

Editorial Advisory Board
Chris Andrews, Mieke Chew, J.M. Coetzee, Lucy Dougan, Lisa Gorton,
Bella Li, Tamara Sampey-Jawad, Suneeta Peres da Costa, Alexis Wright
and Ashleigh Young.

Contact
For editorial enquiries, please email
heat.editor@giramondopublishing.com.
Follow us on Instagram @HEAT.lit and
Twitter @HEAT_journal.

Accessibility
We understand that some formats will not be accessible to all readers.
If you are a reader with specific access requirements, please contact
orders@giramondopublishing.com.

For more information, visit giramondopublishing.com/heat.

Published October 2022
from the Writing and Society Research Centre
at Western Sydney University
by the Giramondo Publishing Company
PO Box 752
Artarmon NSW 1570 Australia
www.giramondopublishing.com

Typeset in Tiempos and Founders Grotesk Condensed
designed by Kris Sowersby at Klim Type Foundry

Printed and bound by Ligare Book Printers
Distributed in Australia by NewSouth Books

A catalogue record for this book is available from
the National Library of Australia.

HEAT Series 3 Number 5
ISBN: 978-1-922725-04-2
ISSN: 1326-1460